What people are saying about...

The Saga of Ike & Penny

Christopher Kimball once again has proven to be one of the most creative financial advisors in the Country. Throughout "The Saga Of Ike and Penny," Chris demonstrates his unique ability to take on the complicated financial issues we all face and simplify them in a most humorous way.

> — *Denis Walsh, CFP®, CFS®, DEP®, RFC®, President and CEO, Money Concepts Capital Corp. LLC*

"Read this book. Chris clearly explains complex financial concepts and presents them in in everyday language anyone can understand."

> — *Mark Anderson, President, The Profit Growth Initiative®*

"If investing seems boring at best and stressful at worst, read this book. It's simple, funny, and makes great points about planning for your financial future!"

> — *Michael Roby, Business Coach, Consultant, and Speaker*

"The problem with personal finance is that it can be so intimidating we'd rather not think about it. But Chris Kimball demystifies it all in an easy-to-understand, fun, and funny book that will make you realize it's not so mysterious after all--- and might even be do-able."

> — *Pat Cashman, National TV and radio personality*

Simple, understandable and enjoyable reading. Follow the financial life journey of Ike and Penny--each storyline is unique and educational.

> — *Dan Burkhalter, Regional Vice-President (retired), Major, International Financial Services Company*

The Saga of
Ike & Penny

Christopher V. Kimball
CFP, MSFS, AEP, CMFC, CLTC, MBS, MDIV

Table of Contents

Table of Contents

INTRODUCTION

Years ago I formed an advisory group to give me advice and counsel on how to improve my practice. One of the members suggested I explain financial concepts to my clients in story form to make what are often complex ideas simpler to understand (thank you, Jack!) I began writing about the imaginary characters you'll meet in this book and found it to be quite enjoyable.

Of course, the world of financial products is unendingly complex, and this book only scratches the surface of some of the most basic investment ideas. My aim is to help demystify a few of the more common products available. More importantly, I hope this book will inspire the reader to do further research so he or she will more clearly understand what is (or should be) a very important part of every person's life.

After all (to quote Zig Ziglar), "Money isn't everything, but it ranks right up there with oxygen!"

— Chris Kimball, *February 28, 2018*

FORWARD

When Chris Kimball asked me to write the foreword to what I choose to call his first book, I found myself assailed by two competing emotions tussling for dominance in my heart. First was dismay. I love my craft of writing but I find it grueling work, and who welcomes extra work? But then, almost immediately, I realized that I was being given a beautiful opportunity of partnering with someone who has been a good friend for many years. So, I read and enjoyed his lovely parable, The Saga of Ike and Penny. What is more, I realized that the wisdom it contained should be widely disseminated.

There are many books filled with important financial information. There are also many books that are easy to read. Very few books are both filled with useful data and are also easy to read. This is one such book. The humor and the human poignancy combine to draw one irresistibly from page to page. Meanwhile, compelling financial truths come catapulting off the page. I wanted to be involved with this book.

My work has always involved teaching how a person's character and values are inseparable from his financial destiny. Does this mean that those of poor character with the wrong values always languish financially? No, of course not; but it is much more likely that they will. Similarly, those of good character with strong values are far more likely to prosper financially. These principles are not only part of Chris Kimball's life but they dart around the story you're about to read like colorful fish in an aquarium. They're small but without them, the entire aquarium is meaningless.

During a Congressional hearing in 1912, famous lawyer, Samuel Untermyer, acting as counsel to the Committee on Banking, insisted to America's leading banker J. P. Morgan, that credit is based upon property or money. Morgan explained that the lawyer had it back to front.

J.P. Morgan: "No, sir; the first thing is character."

Untermeyer: "Before money or property?"

J.P. Morgan: "Before money or anything else. A man I do not trust could not get money from me on all the bonds in Christendom."

I've always assumed that since Untermyer made no secret of his Jewishness, Morgan mischievously dropped in the slightly anachronistic term "Christendom" rather than saying more conventionally, "all the bonds in the world." Morgan and Untermyer had a perfectly cordial relationship and both knew that it was Judeo-Christian values that lay at the heart of America's financial success. Well, not to compare, but Chris and I enjoy far more than merely a cordial relationship. Our deep friendship is, to a large extent, based on a shared reverence for those same values.

And on what else is our friendship based? I could just tell you because I admire men who just get the job done. But that wouldn't be as much fun for me than actually recounting the first of many instances that I saw how Chris' just gets the job done. And perhaps it will be more fun for you too.

You see, there was a time back when we both found ourselves enchanted by model boats. Chris had been wanting to show me his radio-controlled model speed boat. (Yes, we were already two fully grown adult men—I'm sorry but you either get model boats or you don't. That's all there is to it.) Finally, the day arrived. It was a very chilly fall day and I could hardly contain my excitement as I awaited Chris' arrival on the shores of the large lake on which he was going to demonstrate the superb speed and agility of his boat.

It wasn't long before this dashing model speedboat was racing across the waves throwing up an impressive rooster tail of splashing spray. With imperceptible movements of his hands on the radio control, Chris set the model through its paces. Its motor roared a symphony of sound that resonated in my entire body. I was mesmerized. Until, all of a sudden, there was silence; a shocking, unexpected, and worrying silence. A distant two or three hundred yards from shore, the boat's motor had died. I began analyzing our options while the circumstances were being complicated by a cold breeze that had sprung up and which was pushing the boat ever further from where we stood. I had just reached the part of the thought process which dealt with renting a boat in which to pursue the fleeing model, when I realized that Chris had stripped and had dropped into the lake. Oblivious to the cold he struck out for the model in a swift crawl and his fast swimming pace soon closed the distance. Within about ten minutes he was back at the shore pushing the model ahead of him. When his feet found the muddy bottom he rose, and clutching the speedboat, he dressed again. I don't want to say his skin was blue with cold as I don't want to conjure up the picture in any more detail, but I will say that Chris was cold. But he did get the job done. No unnecessary talking and no redundant actions. He just got the job done.

And now, in spite of how terribly difficult it is to write a book, he's gone and got that job done too. And for that, we can all be very grateful because I think his book will enhance your life, just as our friendship has enhanced mine.

— Rabbi Daniel Lapin, *Mercer Island, Washington*

Rabbi Daniel Lapin, known world-wide as America's Rabbi, is a noted rabbinic scholar, best-selling author and host of the Rabbi Daniel Lapin Show. — *www.rabbidaniellapin.com*

Welcome to the financial saga of Ike Matthew Rich and Penny Pincher. I'm basing the financial choices available to Ike and Penny on current law. Some of the approaches I describe weren't available in the past and may not be available in the future. Also, any type of investment, insurance product, or recommendation described is generic in nature and is used for illustrative purposes only—always consult the appropriate professionals before making any financial decisions!

Chapter 1

THE BEGINNING:
SO MANY DECISIONS!

KIDDIE LIFE INSURANCE, 529 PLANS,
ROTH IRAS AND BROKERAGE ACCOUNTS

The families of Ike Matthew Rich and Penny Pincher didn't know each other.

Both Ike and Penny, however, were born in the same year. To their credit, one of the first things the parents considered was how to begin planning for their children's financial future.

Ike's parents, Phil T. Rich and Iwana B. Rich, received a flyer in the mail advertising life insurance for babies. The paperwork was full of words such as "guaranteed" and "promise." There were even pictures included of really cute babies, clearly happy their parents had made the wise decision to purchase life insurance for them.

Penny's parents, Ken I. Pincher and Dona U. Pincher were thinking about college for their little girl, but weren't sure where to start. One of Ken's friends at work, Frank Tok, recommended investing in stocks, while Dona's aunt, Ima Smart, informed her a 529 college savings plan was the best way to go.

Which is the better option? As with so many things in life—it depends. There are advantages and disadvantages in every decision, and each person's situation is different.

For example, if Phil and Iwana love bungee jumping, motorcycle racing, and parachuting from planes, the small, whole life insurance policy might be too conservative for them. It may be true cash value would accumulate over time, but at the conservative, guaranteed rate over 20 years the growth could be far less than an equivalent amount invested in the stock market. Since Phil and Iwana thrive on risk, they might be comfortable with the high volatility inherent in investing in the stock market.

If Ken and Dona like to spend quiet evenings at home, drive a taupe, Ford Taurus, and have never in their respective lives ridden on a roller coaster, investing in the stock market might not be their best choice. If they are in a very high tax bracket, however, the 529 college savings plan might offer them tax advantages, as could the small life insurance policy mentioned earlier (the life insurance policy would undoubtedly experience little or no volatility).

When it comes to tax advantages, 529 plans have some limitations, however. For example, if the money is used for qualifying education expenses, earnings can be accessed tax-free. If, though, the money is distributed and used for, say a new McClaren for Phil, taxes are due on any growth along with a 10% penalty. Although the person who is named to receive the 529 plan's assets can be changed, it needs to be changed to a qualifying relative (IE: natural or legally adopted children, parents, siblings, stepsiblings, stepchildren, stepparents, first cousins, nieces, nephews, aunts or uncles). Plus, the assets need to be used for qualifying-educations costs by the time the beneficiary reaches age 30.

Investing in the stock or bond markets outside a 529 plan can yield diversification and ultimate flexibility for the money's purpose, such as a yacht for Iwana, but unless the investment is in a qualified plan, any realized gains will generally be taxed in the year the gains occurred.

What about using a ROTH IRA for part of the long-term savings? After all, ROTH IRA contributions can generally be withdrawn at any time for any purpose, and investment choices number in the thousands. Couldn't the parents open ROTH IRAs, fund them for 20 years and then take out the contributions to help pay for college, while leaving the growth to grow tax-free for use in retirement? Hmm…

So many choices!

Chapter 2
SHOULD SAVING FOR EDUCATION BE RISKY?
VARIABLE LIFE INSURANCE, AND MORE ABOUT
529 PLANS AND BROKERAGE ACCOUNTS

Phil T. Rich and Iwana B. Rich, and Ken I. Pincher and Dona U. Pincher were trying to decide how to best save for their little darlings' future college expenses.

Phil T. and Iwana B. Rich liked to be aggressive. In fact, they met and fell in love during a World Extreme cage-fighting match.

Because of their propensity for risk, they didn't see the need for being conservative in their college-funding investments. They did, however, like the idea of providing Ike with a life insurance policy. After all, because he was so young, the premiums would be relatively small.

They decided on a two-pronged approach. First, they established and began contributing to a 529 plan which offered a wide choice of investment options. Since they knew it would be 18 years before little Ike would be using money for college, they figured they could invest very aggressively. If the market tanked during the early years, they reasoned there was a pretty good chance it would recover before the college bills started rolling in. Phil's mother-in-law pointed out if Ike took after his father, they might not need the money in 18 years. Or ever.

Both Phil and Iwana were convinced Ike would grow up to be a famous motorcycle stuntman, just like his late uncle Stu "Crash" Pidd. Old "Crash" met an unfortunate end while attempting to jump a row of 47 bulls. (Some said the jump failed because of a malfunction in the electrical system—they had heard Stu was killed due to a horn problem).

Because of the risk in Ike's potential future profession, it was decided Phil would immediately apply for a variable life insurance policy on Ike. The ownership of the policy would transfer from Phil to Ike when Ike turned 21.

The variable policy allowed Phil (and later Ike) to direct the cash value to a number of different investment options which would rise and fall with the stock market. The policy had the potential for more cash value growth than the traditional, whole life insurance policies he had seen, but also carried more investment risk and few guarantees.

Phil and Iwana figured if Ike grew up, never married, and decided he didn't need the life insurance, he could always cash it in and deal with the income tax consequences at that point. (Phil's mother-in-law said she thought the life insurance was unnecessary since if Ike grew up to be anything like his dad, the chance of any woman ever marrying him would be nil).

Ken and Dona were no less enamored with their pride and joy, Penny, but were much more conservative than Phil and Iwana. They decided to take advantage of a state-sponsored 529 plan which allowed them to purchase tuition credits at a current price that guaranteed to cover set amounts of Penny's future tuition costs when she enrolled at an eligible educational institution.

Because they didn't want all their college-funding eggs in one basket, they also opened a standard brokerage account in which to make periodic investments. These funds could be used for college expenses. Or, if Penny grew up to be as brilliant as her grandparents were convinced she would and received a full scholarship to Harvard as her grandparents were convinced she would, the money could be used to buy Penny a new Bentley which her grandparents were convinced she deserved.

To add a bit more flexibility, Ken and Dona each established a ROTH IRA and began contributing the maximum per year. They used a relatively conservative investment allocation, and planned to let the money grow until they retired. They liked the fact that even though they would have to leave any growth in the accounts until age 59 ½, they could take out their contributions without a penalty whenever they wanted (assuming the investment hadn't decreased to less than what they contributed).

Dona was somewhat superstitious, and when Ken broached the subject of life insurance for Penny she burst into tears and refused to even discuss it. She was convinced life insurance on Penny would somehow jinx the youngster and cause her to have a terrible tricycle accident before her second birthday.

Which set of parents made the best choices? That depends on who you ask. Each family's situation is unique. Opinions differ. For example, Phil's mother-in-law was convinced every decision Phil made was completely stupid. But then, she wasn't necessarily objective…

The fact is, different problems required different solutions. Sometimes the *same* problem requires different solutions.

Chapter 3
HIGH SCHOOL, COLLEGE, SPENDING, AND SAVING
DISTRIBUTIONS FROM EDUCATION INVESTMENTS

The years have sped by. Ike and Penny are now in high school.

Ike is enrolled in the public system while Penny's parents opted for a private institution.

Since Ike is one of the "Fighting Acorns" at Washington Jefferson Lincoln Madison Kennedy Public High School, Ike's parents Phil T. and Iwana B. don't have to spend anything on tuition (except the portion of their local taxes allocated to schools).

The fact they opted for public school meant they had some extra money and were able to take exotic vacations, exposing Ike to exciting places around the world. Thanks to these experiences, Ike learned to appreciate the lifestyles of the indigenous peoples of such glamorous locales as Greece, Russia, Italy, China and Forks. He decided he would travel whenever he could. For Ike, experiences trumped security.

Penny's parents, Ken I. and Dona U., however, were concerned about what they perceived as questionable values being espoused at their local, public schools. They enrolled Penny in a private Catholic school known for its strong, faith-based curriculum and large, wooden rulers.

The tuition at the school, St. Harvey of the Bruised Knuckles, was $18,000 per year. The Pinchers felt the money was well-spent, although it didn't leave them much discretionary cash for travel or other luxuries. In fact, Penny spent an inordinate amount of time working on her math assignments because the family had yet to upgrade from its Commodore 64.

Penny's parents often exchanged knowing smiles, however, because for Penny's high-school graduation they were planning on surprising her with a slightly-used laptop equipped with a state-of-the-art email system called Juno. She would be so thrilled!

During Ike and Penny's junior year of high school, both sets of parents had the foresight to begin looking into opportunities for college financial aid. Ever since Ike was a tyke, his parents had been aggressive with their investment choices in the 529 plan and variable life insurance policy, so both vehicles had accumulated significant assets. Fortunately, most colleges don't count life insurance cash values against financial aid, and 529 assets can be viewed more favorably than a straight savings account, too. In the final analysis, Ike was able to qualify for some financial aid as well as federal student loans.

Ike's parents decided to use the 529 plan along with cash flow to fund college expenses, leaving the life insurance cash value to accumulate tax-deferred to be used in case of an emergency. They avoided using the available loans, even though payments wouldn't be required until Ike graduated. The interest rates seemed high, and besides, their choice to invest aggressively happened to work out well.

Penny's parents used the 529 plan to cover a considerable amount of Penny's college costs, although they did withdraw some of the contributions they had made to their ROTH IRAs over the years. They were careful not to withdraw any of the earnings, though, since if withdrawn before age 59 ½, ROTH earnings are generally subject to taxes and a penalty.

Also available were funds in Ken's traditional IRA. Even though any proceeds withdrawn would be fully taxable if the money was used to pay for college, the 10% premature withdrawal penalty would not apply—even though Ken was younger than 59 ½.

The brokerage account they opened to help pay for Penny's college had, unfortunately, been drained years earlier when Penny became involved in the equestrian hobby. She received a pony for her 16th Christmas, and discovered horses eat a lot of expensive hay.

Ike enrolled in the well-known, state school, Keggers University. He decided to major in medieval history, despite the fact his vocational test scores indicate a proclivity for nursing.

Penny chose a private, religious university which was much more expensive than the state schools. By living at home during the school year, however, she saved enough money so four years' worth of tuition still managed to fit into her budget. She researched average income levels of various professions and decided to major in anesthesiology. At first, she was shocked by the amount of homework required to finish the program, but she soon became numb to it.

Both Ike and Penny understood the power of compounding interest, but only Penny took the initiative to open a ROTH IRA. She only worked part time during her college years, but was able to invest $5,500 (the maximum allowed for those under 50) of her earnings in the ROTH IRA each year.

Ike spent any money he earned on parts for his motorcycle and what he called "liquid nourishment."

Penny maintained a 4.00 GPA throughout her university career, while Ike eked out a 2.2.

During their senior year of college, Ike and Penny met. Penny was working as a volunteer, planting a vegetable garden in a poor neighborhood. Ike happened to be riding his motorcycle in the same part of town. Ike took a corner a bit too fast, hit the curb, and ended up face down in the radishes. Fortunately, he was wearing a helmet, and after brushing the roots from his face, the first thing he saw was Penny. Even though Penny knew Ike's motorcycle insurance rates would skyrocket if he made a claim for the damage due to his careless driving, she was somehow enamored with Ike and his radish-filled leather jacket.

They began dating, and soon things began to look serious. As time went by, talk of marriage, a home, and a family began finding its way into their conversations.

Finally, Penny told Ike it was time to sit down and have a serious conversation about their future goals. Ike agreed, and the planning began.

Chapter 4
THE JOYS OF MARRIAGE
AND FINDING A FINANCIAL PLANNER

At first, Ike was nervous about marriage. Once his head fully cleared from the motorcycle accident, he began considering the full ramifications of making that kind of commitment. If he settled down and started a family, he might have to forego some or all of his expensive habits: fast motorcycles, fast cars, fast computers, and fast women.

Still, he reasoned, two people can live cheaper than one. If he could convince Penny to pursue her career in anesthesiology, it's quite possible he could continue or even expand his hobbies (except for the fast women, of course). Plus, if they had children it would only be a few years until the kids would be old enough to start doing housework, yardwork, and other menial tasks (which Ike assumed was the purpose of having children). This would give him even more free time.

Yes, this marriage and family idea just kept looking better and better!

Penny had her own thoughts about joining with Ike in holy matrimony. She was planning on working in the medical field for a few years, but she was more interested in staying home and raising children than working her way up the financial-success ladder. She wanted security and a stable life. That's why during a candlelit, romantic dinner she brought up the subject of insurance.

Ike had big plans too, but rather than financial security, they had more to do with the immediate opportunities which he hoped would follow the romantic dinner. Nevertheless, because he didn't want to ruin the mood, Ike listened intently as Penny explained her concerns.

She worried about what would happen if once they married one or both of them became sick or had an accident preventing them from working. How would they pay their bills?

Once they became accustomed to living on two incomes, she was unsure what would happen if one of them died and the other became financially strapped. She realized that once they began having children, the problem would become even worse.

What about medical insurance, car insurance, and homeowners insurance?

Should they start saving for their retirement? If so, how should they start?

Was it too early to start saving for college for their future children, even though it might be years before they were born?

What about their aging parents, Phil T. Rich, Iwana B. Rich, Ken I. Pincher, and Dona U. Pincher? Who would take care of them when they needed care?

Penny was anxious to address all these subjects before heading to the altar.

As mentioned, Ike listened intently to Penny's words. At least, he listened intently through the first two sentences. At that point, his eyes glazed over and he began staring at the desert menu. The key lime pie looked delicious.

When Penny finished talking, Ike snapped out of his stupor and mumbled he would look into it, not exactly sure what "it" was.

Despite his promise, the busyness of life got in the way of Ike's research and no progress was made to address Penny's insecurities. During that time, however, Ike's motorcycle received a new paint job, and his hot-rod sported a new Holley 750 cfm carburetor. As happens with so many people, the urgent and unimportant took precedent over the important but not urgent.

Then something happened.

Ike's best friend, Robert Forapples (his friends called him Bob), was taking his morning walk through the park, when suddenly a teenager's remote-controlled airplane lost its radio signal and careened into Bob's head, killing him instantly.

Bob had a wife and two children, but no life insurance. Because Bob had been the primary breadwinner, his wife and kids lost their home and had to move in with Bob's weird uncle, Owen Monee. Owen had always struggled to keep his financial head above water, and providing for three more people certainly wouldn't make things easier.

As Ike watched the tragedy unfold, two thoughts struck him like bolts of lightning. First, the teenager should have used a better transmitter. Second, maybe he had better take the subject of risk management a little more seriously.

He immediately began looking for a financial planner.

He had heard it was a good idea to work with a planner with the CFP designation, although he wasn't sure why. He thought maybe the acronym stood for Crazy, Fun People, and was a bit disappointed when he discovered the real meaning, Certified Financial Planner. He went to the Financial Planning Association's website and located a planner in his neighborhood.

Ike made an appointment to visit the planning firm of Weewil, Dewitt and Well.

When he arrived, the first thing Ike told them was he wanted some life insurance. He was surprised when the planner told him that wasn't the first thing he needed.

Chapter 5

PROTECTING THE BREADWINNER'S BREAD

DISABILITY INCOME INSURANCE

Since he had already purchased home and car insurance, Ike felt as if he was an insurance genius. He was surprised, therefore, when the financial planner, Lotta Branes, told him the next risk he should address wasn't life insurance. After all, Ike's favorite movie during his college days (or at least what he could remember of them—college for Ike was a bit of a blur) featured a character named Ned Ryerson. According to Ned, a life insurance policy was the ultimate acquisition. This seemed reasonable to Ike, especially considering some of the risky behaviors in which he liked to participate.

Nevertheless, Lotta explained that the lifestyle Ike enjoyed was far more likely to result in an injury than death. In fact, Lotta said Ike's chance of becoming disabled before age 65 was at least 6 times that of dying!

"It's not that life insurance isn't important," Lotta told him, "but when building a financial strategy, it's prudent to address the most probable risks first."

Lotta suggested that at the same time Ike applied for

a disability-income insurance policy, he and Penny should begin building an emergency fund which could cover least four months' worth of expenses. Doing these two things would help, should Ike become too sick or injured to work.

Over the years, Ike had thought of death many times. For example, as he left the seat of his motorcycle and headed toward the cement at 100 miles-per-hour, he thought of death. As he felt his tires lose their grip on a hairpin turn, he thought of death. Even as a child, as he jumped from the roof clinging to his umbrella--only then to realize Mary Poppins wasn't real--he thought of death. But disability? It never crossed his mind.

As Lotta described the various features, benefits and exclusions found in disability-income insurance policies, Ike's eyes began to glaze over (a frequent problem for Ike). His imagination began painting a frightening picture: he saw Penny spoon-feeding him a mouthful of goopy mush made from vegetables and sausage as he tried not to face-plant into the bowl. Penny had quit her job to take care of him. With no income, they lost their home and were forced to move into Uncle Owen Monee's woodshed (Bob Forapples and his family were still using the guest room). Ike's injuries had left him paralyzed. He wasn't as young as he used to be, why didn't he think before entering that breakdancing contest? From the corner of his eye, he saw a rat scurrying toward his foot. He felt the beast clawing its way up his trouser leg, but was unable to do anything about it...

Lotta was just coming to the "assumed close" portion of her presentation, saying, "Can you think of any reason you wouldn't want to apply for this insurance policy today?" when Ike was overcome by his phantasm.

"NOOOOOO!" he screamed as he snapped back to reality.

"Good," said Lotta," then please sign here, and I'll take the check for the first two months' worth of coverage.

When Ike got home and told Penny about their new monthly bill, he was surprised that instead of a glare, she gave him a hug. Penny knew, despite what Ike thought, Ike's biggest asset was his ability to make money. Not insuring that would be dumber than riding a motorcycle naked (something Ike promised her he would never do again).

Penny was glad the first step toward financial security had been taken, but she knew this was just the beginning.

Chapter 6
TAKING THE LONG VIEW
LONG-TERM-CARE INSURANCE

Newlyweds I. M. Rich and Penny Pincher-Rich (Penny was old-fashioned, but not quite old-fashioned enough not to hyphenate her last name) were settling down into the honeymoon period of their young marriage (that's when you still think your spouse is perfect, you have no kids, no pets, little-to-no-debt, and the husband doesn't yet burp in front of the wife). One day, they received a disturbing phone call.

Ike's Dad, Phil T. Rich had been roller skating with his wife Iwana B. Rich, when he tried his famous "shoot the duck" move and accidentally careened into the concession stand. Much to the horror of the onlookers, the force of Phil hitting the wall simultaneously dislodged the hot chocolate dispenser and the Slushee machine. Before he could say "bilateral balance," scalding milk cascaded onto his left ear and frozen sugar-water flooded his right.

This unfortunate turn of events caused the earwax in his left ear to melt and the earwax in his right ear to solidify. The resulting imbalance caused Ike to contract a rare brain disease called Waxingis Poeticus. From that moment forward, Ike could only speak Lewis Carroll poetry—in other words, what he said was impossible to decipher.

Iwana was distraught. She and Phil had only just begun to enjoy retirement and hadn't even had time to look through the brochures they had accumulated from Florida, Arizona, Hawaii, Mexico and Holland America. Now, Phil would need 24-hour-per-day care. Iwana wasn't sure she could deal with the situation alone, Phil had always been very independent and determined. Trying to corral him would be no easy task; Iwana was a petite woman, after all. Phil, on the other hand, was huge. He was so large that he had to get baptized at Sea World.

Iwana decided Phil needed professional care. She was astounded to find that 24-hour, in-home care would cost $8,000 per month! With the help of the calculator on her smart phone, it didn't take her long to figure out the annual amount was close to $100,000.

She immediately met with a qualified estate-planning attorney to consider her options. The attorney, I. "Bill" Howerly, said because she and Phil had done no long-term-care planning, they would have to spend down the vast majority of their assets before they would be eligible to receive any Governmental financial assistance. Son and daughter-in-law Ike and Penny were basically broke, so they couldn't help, either.

Iwana had no choice but to begin using savings to pay for the care Phil so desperately needed. Plus, if Iwana had to hear "The Jabberwocky" one more time, she knew she would go as insane as Phil.

Meanwhile, as Ike began to see his inheritance disappear before his very eyes, Penny determined not to make the same mistake as her parents-in-law. She dragged Ike back to the financial planner, Lotta Branes, at the planning firm of Weewil, Dewitt and Well.

Lotta had taken courses in long-term-care insurance and consequently had the designation CLTC (Certified in Long-Term Care). She carefully explained to Ike and Penny how long-term-care insurance works. Penny was interested in the fact she could purchase daily or monthly benefits for future long-term-care expenses which could be indexed for inflation. This would increase the benefit amount to help keep up with rising medical-care costs. She was told how, in order to receive benefits, she or Ike would either have to be unable to perform two of six "activities of daily living," or suffer from severe cognitive problems.

One of the activities of daily living triggers was incontinence. When Ike heard that, he piped up about the time he experienced that very phenomenon when going around a hairpin turn at 80 miles-per-hour in a 1965 Corvair. Penny asked Lotta if Ike's comment would be considered evidence of cognitive-impairment.

Although the premiums for the long-term-care insurance policies Ike and Penny purchased were relatively expensive—Ike kept grumbling he could buy a brand-new Kawasaki Ninja 650 every year with the money they were spending on the premiums—Penny patiently explained that if in 40 years they each needed only five years of long-term care, that could easily be the equivalent of purchasing 310 of the same motorcycle—even indexed for inflation!

Ike had to admit Penny had a point. Besides, even if he wasn't able to ride motorcycles in 40 years, he had some great ideas about V-8-powered wheelchairs. Plus, having long-term-care insurance pay for some or all of their long-term-care expenses could allow a substantial amount of assets being left to their future children. The thought of children got Ike thinking about making children, and once again his eyes began to glaze over...

The thought of Ike involved with lightweight, high-powered vehicles got Penny thinking about life insurance. Could she possibly get Ike to visit Lotta Branes yet again?

Chapter 7
A MATTER OF LIFE AND DEATH
LIFE INSURANCE

Penny had begun to worry about yet another depressing subject: death.

Specifically, Ike's death.

Penny recalled from her Sunday-school training that only a couple of people in history had managed to escape death, and since Ike was no prophet, she was pretty sure he was eventually going to meet his Maker in the conventional way. Based on how he lived, she feared that day might be sooner rather than later.

If Ike did shuffle off this mortal coil earlier than expected, Penny realized his income would be gone as well, leaving her in a precarious financial position. She began researching life insurance on the internet and found an inestimable amount of conflicting information.

Confused, she decided to seek the advice of an insurance agent. Looking through the yellow pages, she found a life insurance agent with a name that sounded vaguely familiar. She decided to call him and make an appointment.

The next day, the knock on the door confirmed Ned Ryerson had arrived with his briefcase full of ideas.

Ned was a tall, thin, enthusiastic man with a smile that showed more teeth than it should, and a handshake that was vigorous and lasted a little too long. He began pulling out charts and graphs, effusing about the features and benefits of every product available from The Strongarm American Eagle in God We Trust Insurance Company of America (headquartered in Shuqualak, Mississippi). Of course, the fine print explained the company was in no way affiliated with or endorsed by the US Government.

In what seemed to Penny to be an unending stream of consciousness, Ned described annually-increasing term insurance, level term insurance, return-of-premium term insurance, term insurance riders, universal life insurance, guaranteed universal life insurance, variable life insurance, modified whole life insurance, modified variable whole life insurance, variable universal life insurance, single-premium life insurance, paid-up at 65 life insurance, participating whole life insurance, non-participating whole life insurance, waiver of premium, double-indemnity, dividends, mortality rates, mortality assumptions, cost-per-thousand expenses, investment fees and expenses, the IRS MEC rules, transfer-for-value, tax preferences enjoyed by life insurance, loans, surrender charges, cash surrender value, 1035 exchanges, and a description of interpolated terminal reserve.

Needless to say, by the time Ned was finished, Penny's head was spinning.

"I'll have to think about it," she mumbled.

Ned tried his best to close the deal, but even his best tie-down questions, alternate-advance offers, and objection-overcoming skills couldn't move Penny to action.

He left, assuring Penny he'd check back in a few days.

When Ike got home that afternoon, Penny tried her best to share her newfound life insurance knowledge, but all Ike heard was a confused mass of gobbledygook.

Once again, they met with Lotta Branes.

Lotta explained there were basically two types of life insurance; one which was intended to be in force temporarily (term insurance), and the other designed to remain in force until the death of the person insured (whole life insurance). From these two types, all others had developed.

Ike and Penny learned most term insurance had no cash value, lasted for 10, 15, 20, or in some cases 30 years, and only stayed in force as long as the premiums were paid or until the end of the term, whichever came first.

Whole life and universal life, however, could build cash value inside the policy which in some cases could be accessed before death, could last until age 100 or beyond (or the death of the insured), but usually cost substantially more than term insurance.

Lotta brought up another good point: Penny was hoping she and Ike would start a family soon. If Penny died after children had come into the picture, Ike would need money to either hire someone to watch the kids, or to provide him income if he decided to stay home full- or part-time.

Penny liked the idea of having something permanent, but knew she and Ike couldn't afford all permanent life insurance—at least not at this point in their lives. After working with Lotta, they decided to purchase a combination of permanent and term insurance, based on the analysis Lotta provided. The policies also included a "waiver of premium" feature, which meant if either Ike or Penny became disabled, the premiums for his or her life insurance policy would be paid by the insurance company until a full recovery had been made.

Once the coverage was in force, Penny felt great.

Ike felt like a hamburger and a shake, but then, he was always hungry.

A few years went by, and Penny heard a sound that seemed to grow louder with each passing day. It was her biological clock.

Ike had trouble hearing anything because in high school he spent too much time blasting Led Zeppelin through his Sansui speakers (with 15" woofers).

Finally, Penny confronted Ike.

"It's time we had kids," she demanded.

"You're such a kid--der," he replied, trying to deflect Penny's statement with a joke.

Penny was not amused.

Her frustration had been growing over the last couple of years, and now it was crunch time. Ike's thick-headed response to her plea pushed her to the breaking point.

"I can't take it anymore," she sobbed. "If you don't want a family, then I don't want to be married to you."

Ike was stunned (actually, Ike had spent most of his life stunned). His first thought was, "I wonder how much this is going to cost me...?"

Neither wanted to make a snap decision about something so important, however, so they made an appointment with a collaborative law, financial-planning professional, Mae Kitwork, to discuss the financial ramifications of divorce.

Chapter 8
THE MARRIAGE GETS ROCKY
CAN YOU AFFORD A DIVORCE?

Penny had wanted kids for as long as she could remember.

When she was only four, her parents gave her a Chatty-Kathy doll for Christmas. Penny loved that doll. It had a string coming from the back of its neck that when pulled, caused the doll to talk (that was the chatty part).

While playing mommy, she pulled the string so many times the doll's voice box malfunctioned. From then on, the only things Kathy could chat were two utterances which sounded like "roast" and "carrot" although no one could be sure exactly what the doll was trying to say.

Penny couldn't wait to get married and have real children (preferably with more than a two-word vocabulary).

Growing up, Ike spent a lot of time with his five female cousins. They played with dolls, too, each with its own special features. Beautiful Crissy had a large hole in its head from which hair could be extended (that doll got a haircut from its young owner, leaving only the hole). Baby Boo made realistic crying noises (until Ike jammed a pencil down its throat which, ironically, stopped the crying). Baby Pattaburp, although cute, belched (this was the only doll Ike thought had any redeeming quality). Baby Fun didn't burp, but instead blew bubbles (which stained the carpet, the sofa, and the cat). Finally, Ike's least favorite was a doll named Annie. Its sole talent was wetting its diaper (Ike disliked this doll the most; probably because it reminded him of his own bedwetting problems).

Ike was traumatized by this exposure to so many cacophonous baby dolls. His ambivalence toward youngsters only became more pronounced when a 14-year-old neighbor shot a hole through Ike's garage door window with a sling-shot. He told himself he would never bring such trouble into the world by procreating.

Ike and Penny's divergent opinions of children collided when Penny heard the alarm from her biological clock. No longer satisfied to hit the snooze button yet again, she confronted Ike.

"If you won't father my children, I'll find someone who will."

Ike grudgingly turned off the Survivor rerun he was watching. "Are you sure artificial insemination is the answer? I've heard that's expensive."

"No, you idiot," she sobbed, "I'm talking about divorce! I've made an appointment with a financial planner who works with divorcing couples. Her name is Mae Kitwork and I insist we see her together."

"Oh, great" thought Ike, "the only thing worse than listening to a financial planner drone on and on is listening to one droning about divorce."

Nevertheless, he agreed. He knew if he didn't, Penny would keep crying and he would miss the rest of Survivor.

A week later they were in Mae's office.

Mae Kitwork was a Certified Financial Planner practitioner who specialized in helping divorcing couples equitably divide up their assets. She was very good at her job, but always maintained the hope that during her meetings with clients she could convince them to patch things up and stay married.

The first thing Mae did was take an inventory of Ike and Penny's assets. This included retirement accounts such as IRAs, ROTH IRAs, 401(k) and 403(b) plans, as well as investments in taxable brokerage accounts.

Next, the value of their home, cars, and other household items were tallied.

Finally, Ike and Penny each determined monthly budgets (assuming they were living separately), and compared them with their respective incomes.

Since the house purchase was relatively recent and the crash of '08 decimated its value, there was no equity—in fact, they were underwater by $100,000. There was no debt on the cars, however, and Ike's motorcycles were also free and clear. Ike had a Roth IRA with a value of $90,000, a traditional IRA of $90,000, and he had just rolled his 401(k) balance from his previous employer into his new employer's plan; it totaled $150,000.

Ike had three motorcycles: 1) 2008 MV Agusta F4CC worth $120,000, 2) 2010 Vyrus 987 C3 4V worth $104,000, and 3) 1968 Suzuki ST-12 worth $79.

Even though their cars were community property, Ike tended to use the 2015 Corvette Z06 (value: $83,000) while Penny preferred the 2000 Toyota Prius (value: $2,500)

Penny had a traditional IRA worth $69,000 and a 403(b) plan balance of $50,000. She also owned a Quattro sewing machine valued at $9,000 and a set of antique dolls she inherited from her grandmother worth $10,000 (the dolls were worth $10,000, not the grandmother).

They also had investments worth $100,000 in a taxable brokerage account held at the firm of Byhi - Sello - Orr - Else.

Ike's new job as a Baskin Robbins ice cream taster paid him well, $150,000 per year plus bonuses, not to mention all the ice cream he could eat.

Penny worked part-time for a local elementary school in the special education department. It was gratifying work, although demanding, and only provided $20,000 of annual income. She did have the summers free, though, which gave her a chance to enjoy her hobby of quilting expansive wall-hangings depicting Elvis cavorting with Marilyn Monroe in front of a '50s diner. Penny had even pioneered a new quilting technique; sewing LEDs into the quilt to illuminate the taillights of the pink, '59 Cadillac.

Although Ike and Penny's total income was $170,000 per year—in the top 10% of income earners in America—as is the case with so many Americans, they spent virtually all of it as soon as it was earned. The exception was their retirement plan contributions. They were taken out of their paychecks before Ike or Penny could get their hands on the money!

Not only did Ike and Penny enjoy spending every last cent they took home, Ike enjoyed spending more than they were taking home. His penchant for fast cars and rare motorcycles racked up $40,000 in credit card debt.

Ike wasn't worried about the credit cards, though; he figured the statements showed the cards were paying him 27.9% annual interest…

The first thing Mae did was total the assets, income and expenses.

Including the value of their retirement plans, vehicles, and household goods, Ike and Penny's net worth was about $750,000.

After retirement contributions and taxes, their take-home pay was $9,000 per month.

Ike thought $9,000 per month sounded great. He immediately started thinking about the new Harley-Davidson he'd be driving soon.

His Harley-Davidson thoughts were driven from his mind, however, when Mae revealed their expenses were $9,500 per month.

"What about all that interest I'm getting from my credit cards? I'll bet that helps!" Ike declared.

Penny rolled her eyes while Mae patiently explained credit card interest was a cost, not a benefit.

While Ike was processing this newly-revealed knowledge, Mae gave them the really bad news.

"$9,500 per month is what you're spending together. If you were to divorce, in order to maintain your standard of living you would each need $6,700 per month of net income. This means if you divorce and live separately you will have a deficit of $4,400 per month."

"Wait…" Mae paused, "I just realized if you file your taxes as single individuals you'll probably have a higher tax burden, so things could be even worse than we thought."

This information bludgeoned Ike just as he was just beginning to come to terms with the fact their credit cards were creating over $900 per month in interest debt.

Although Penny viewed Ike as an insensitive Neanderthal, as his head began wobbling and beads of sweat formed on his brow, she almost felt sorry for him.

"It's OK, honey, we have a lot of money saved for retirement."

Mae's brow furrowed, "Actually, your investments and savings only total $549,000, of which $359,000 is taxable. Even if we use QDROs to help you access your taxable accounts without penalties, after taxes—we'll assume 22%—your total retirement and savings equal about $470,000. Subtracting your credit card debt and assuming you sell your home and take the $100,000 loss; that leaves around $330,000. If we split that amount evenly and the funds earn 5% per year, this only generate less than $700 per month for each of you; far less than the $4,400-per-month you need."

Penny's head was spinning. As the full financial ramifications of divorce began sinking in, she could feel tears running down her cheeks and falling on her shoes (she was sitting in the lotus position).

"What's a QDRO?" she wailed.

QDRO is pronounced quadro, so at this point, Ike piped up, "That's what the Beach Boys sang about in 409. Dual quadros!"

Mae and Penny both rolled their eyes.

"Ike," Mae explained, "QDRO stands for a qualified domestic relations order."

Anything to do with marital relations interested Ike, but he was still confused.

"A QDRO allows one spouse to access the other's retirement plan, usually without any kind of premature withdrawal penalty, although this doesn't apply to IRAs. Since you have more in your retirement plan than Penny, you may have to give her some of those funds."

"Could I just give her one of my motorcycles instead?" Ike asked.

"It's not as simple as that," answered Mae, "in fact, things can get pretty complicated. We have a lot of work to do."

Chapter 9
NO, YOU CAN'T AFFORD IT!
A CREDIT CAROL

Financial planner Mae Kitwork had shown Ike and Penny their true financial situation. They spent more than they earned, they had $40,000 of credit card debt, and things would only get worse (especially for Penny) if they divorced.

"Tell me more about that quad-copter thing," Ike inquired, "didn't you say that would give us money without taxes?"

"It's a QDRO," Mae explained patiently, "and it stands for Qualified Domestic Relations Order. It won't eliminate taxes, but it could allow you to access certain retirement funds without the IRS 10% premature distribution penalty."

Ike didn't particularly like the word "mature."

He took a deep breath. "How does it work?"

"Well," Mae said, "in your case, we could assign your $150,000 401(k) plan to Penny, and her $50,000 403(b) to you. Even though neither of you is 59 ½ yet, you could immediately access the $50,000 and Penny the $150,000 without a penalty, although you would still have to pay income tax on whatever you took out."

Penny thought that sounded pretty good—especially the part about her getting $150,000 and Ike getting $50,000.

"What gives?" Ike exclaimed, "Why should Penny get three times as much as me?"

"I, it's I! I!" exclaimed Penny (grammar was never Ike's strong suit).

"Who are you--Scotty?" he shot back.

"Settle down," demanded Mae, "Ike, if you take a look at what each of you own, after an assumed 22% tax hit but ignoring any tax penalties, your assets are about $586,000; Penny's are only $112,000. Even if we assigned your 401(k) balance to her and she kept her 403(b), you'd still have over a quarter-of-a-million dollars more than she'd have."

"It's not my fault Penny couldn't figure out motorcycles are more valuable than sewing machines," he muttered.

The bigger issue, of course, wasn't the relative value of sewing machines, motorcycles or doll collections—it was the monthly deficit in the household budget, and the fact divorcing would only make things worse.

In what seemed far less than 50 minutes, the session with Mae was over. All Ike and Penny could do was go home and think about their unappealing options.

That night, Ike slept fitfully. Tossing and turning, he was suddenly awakened by a strange sound. Struggling to focus he noticed a shape in the corner of the room. Gradually he recognized the apparition as his high-school economics teacher, a Pakistani gentleman named Yueshud Saevit.

"Mr. Saevit—is that you? How did you get here? What does this mean? I thought you died in a Yak accident back in 2005!"

Ike heard a voice he remembered, "Ike, Ike, Ike. You are just as thick as you were in high school. The reason I was even in the vicinity of a Yak was that I squandered my wealth and had to go back to Pakistan and take over my family's Yak-herding business."

"Yak herding?"

"I know, it's not glamorous, there are flies, and there's no tenure, either."

"But what happened? How did you blow all your money?"

Yueshud shook his translucent head from side to side, "Ice cream. It was ice cream. Little things at first; a single-scoop sundae, maybe a small, soft-serve cone during lunch, you know, just something to take the edge off my hunger. But then, things began to change. It went from one scoop to two, then three, then to banana splits, giant chocolate milkshakes, and the malts—oh, the malts! I couldn't live without them. I began visiting Baskin Robbins two, sometimes three times every day."

"Why are you telling me this?" Ike inquired.

"Don't you see? I ate more than I could afford! I had to take on a second job just to pay the interest on the huge balances on my credit cards. Have you seen the price of ice cream lately? In the end, I had to declare bankruptcy. I was so ashamed I had no choice but to leave my teaching career (after all, what kind of an example was I to the children?) I stowed away on a freighter to Pakistan, and, well, you know the rest. Ike, I don't want what has happened to me to happen to you. I'm condemned to roam--ice cream-less--throughout eternity. I know math was never your strong suit, but something in your financial life has got to change."

Yueshud's pleading sent chills down Ike's spine.

Ike's voice trembled, "What do I have to do?"

"Tonight, you will be visited by three spirits: The ghost of credit report past, the ghost of credit report present, and the ghost of credit report future. The first will visit when the clock strikes one."

"Is there any way they could all show up at once? Penny always tells me uninterrupted sleep is important for good skin tone."

"NO!" Yueshud insisted, "the sprits will appear exactly at their appointed times. Being late, as you will discover, is never a good thing—especially when it comes to money. Now I must go. You're not the only couple in the Country with money problems, you know. I've got a lot more houses to visit."

With that, the image of Yueshud Saevit vanished in a puff of whipped cream.

Despite the adrenaline which filled his veins, Ike rested his head on his pillow and began drifting off to sleep.

"What just happened?" he wondered, "I must have imagined that entire thing. Maybe it was just a bout of indigestion from the dreamsicle ice cream pie I had for dinner." Within moments, he was snoring.

Soon, Ike was again roused, but this time it was the sound of a tiny, Harley-Davidson motorcycle coming from his officially-licensed Harley-Davidson motorcycle cuckoo clock.

Through his blurry eyes he saw the miniature Wide-Glide move in and out of the tiny barn, the doors opening and closing in concert with the movement of the tiny icon of America.

Then, very unexpectedly, the little doors opened again. From the opening wafted what looked to be the kind of mist Ike's high school rock band created during performances by using dry ice (it made his group look groovy).

This mist, however, wasn't at all groovy. It coalesced into the form of a dollar bill, and to Ike's amazement, the face of George Washington began to speak.

"Ike, I'd like to show you something."

"Who are you?" Ike exclaimed.

"I am the ghost of credit report past. Look deeply into my eyes and tell me what you see."

Ike stared at the spirit, but nothing happened.

"Am I supposed to see something special? I don't see anything but you," protested Ike.

"Try this," the spirit replied, "stare at one, particular point and focus on only that. Let me know if you still don't see anything. It's like those posters they sell at the fair; you know the ones--if you look at them long enough you see the Mona Lisa."

Ike stared.

All at once, the middle of the dollar-bill-shaped spirit seemed to open. Ike could see a vision of himself standing in a showroom surrounded by shiny, new motorcycles.

"Of course, you can afford it," he heard the salesman say, "we can get this beauty in your garage for only $350 per month."

Ike watched himself respond, "Sounds great. After all, I work hard. I deserve this awesome bike! It will look so cool next to my other two."

"Of course it will," crooned the salesman, preparing to use the alternate advance closing technique. "Would you prefer to use your Visa or MasterCard?"

Ike was signing the purchase agreement as the vision ended.

"But, but, it was only $350 per month!" stammered Ike.

"Yes," answered the spirit, "but it is debt—on a depreciating asset, no less."

Ike fidgeted.

"Behold, another vision," the spirit announced, and the inside of a lavish casino came into view.

"Hey, that was last year at Harrah's!" Ike crowed.

As the words left his lips Ike realized he shouldn't be celebrating what he was seeing.

"Yes," the spirit agreed, "it was. You lost $4,500 gambling during that vacation."

"If Penny hadn't stopped me, I could have won it all back."

Only after he had spoken the words did he realize how ridiculous he sounded.

"I think we've seen enough," announced the spirit, "but stay vigilant, for you will soon be visited again."

The dollar began to shrink into the darkness, and was gone.

Ike was indignant. "I'll bet that stupid spirit has never hit triple digits at 9,000 RPMs on a smooth, country road. What does he know about the relative value of experience?"

Before Ike could think of another rationalization, the miniature motorcycle again appeared, motor revving, but this time it traveled in and out twice. Ike knew what that meant, another visit.

Sure enough, the window began to glow, waver and change shape; elongating and stretching to form a thin, golden rectangle.

"Ike!" the form bellowed.

"Now what?" Ike felt his throat getting dry.

"I am the ghost of credit report present."

"You look like a bar of gold."

"That's the idea."

"Oh spirit," Ike tried his best to sound humble—quite a challenge--"what will you show me?"

"Observe," commanded the gold-bar-shaped spirit.

Ike watched the bedroom wall illuminate, as if it were a big-screen plasma TV (but without the lag that drives gamers crazy).

The scene depicted on the wall was Ike and Penny talking with a contractor.

"There's no need to wait," the contractor assured them, "we can have the hot tub installed in less than two weeks, and with our nothing-down, zero-interest-for-two-years, factory-rebate, no-risk-guarantee, money-back-no-questions-asked policy, you can invest in this wonderful addition to your home right now!"

"Hey, that was yesterday," Ike protested. "You said you were the ghost of credit report present."

"Listen, buddy," the spirit scolded, "that's as close as we can get to present. I mean, think about it; if all I could show you was the actual present—what is happening at this very second--all we'd see is me talking to you. I don't care how you try to fit this into quantum physics, but to make this whole 'ghostly-vision' thing work, you're going to have to work with me a little."

Ike began to wish he'd stayed awake during his philosophy class so he could offer a stiff rejoinder. Instead, he just nodded.

"Sorry."

The spirit continued, "OK, watch this."

The image changed to a car dealership; Ike was talking with an attractive saleswoman.

"Wait," Ike said raising his hand, "that was two days ago. That's even less 'present' than…"

Ike's voice trailed off. He realized belaboring the point would only extend this painful experience.

"Did you say something?" the spirit asked.

"No."

"I didn't think so. Now, pay attention!"

The saleswoman was standing a little closer to Ike than necessary. Ike didn't seem to mind, and tried giving the impression he was actually hearing her words.

"Your car is almost five years old," she oozed, "things will start breaking. Don't you think it would be safer for your wife to have reliable transportation? Besides, we have the latest hybrid- sports-mini-van in stock. It has a ten-star crash-safety rating and over 500 horsepower. A woman needs power to avoid accidents."

"Sure," the Ike in the vision replied, "but I don't have that kind of cash right now."

"No problem! If we give you $1000 trade-in on your old car, you won't even need a down payment. You'll only need to make a monthly investment of $450 in your new vehicle."

"Sure. Safety is important. Power is good." Ike in the vision suddenly inhaled sharply to recapture a bit of drool dribbling from his mouth.

Real Ike felt his face flush. "Alright!" he complained, "I've seen enough."

"Oh, no. You haven't seen enough" said the spirit. "You will be visited once more, and your final visitor will show you things too dark for me to mention; such things as credit scores that make bankers quake with fear."

With that, the spirit was gone.

As predicted, when the mini-Harley revved up, a third apparition appeared.

Rising from the floor, this spirit was darker than the previous ghosts, and took the form of a huge, well-worn Susan B. Anthony dollar.

"Don't tell me, you must be the ghost of credit report yet to come."

The coin said nothing, but slowly spun one revolution.

"What—you're not going to say anything? This reminds me of a Charles Dickens story."

The coin seemed to become angry (although one must admit, discerning emotion from a coin can be tricky, especially if the coin is female).

Without making a sound, the coin projected a holographic image of an attorney's office. A surprisingly realistic Penny doppelganger was crying softly as the family attorney spoke.

"Penny, I'm so sorry for your loss. You must feel terrible. How were you to know that Ike riding his motorcycle on the freeway during an ice storm might be a little risky? You don't have any experience riding motorcycles, after all. If you had, I'm sure you wouldn't have recommended it."

"The problem," he continued, "is that while Ike was alive, you both overspent. You've missed house payments, defaulted on credit cards, and to make matters worse, Ike never made a will. I hate to be the one to tell you this, but you'll have to live the rest of your life with Ike's mother."

"Oh, NO!" Penny sobbed.

The vision faded.

Gradually, another scene appeared. It was the very motorcycle dealership where Ike had purchased his last two bikes. Two salesmen were laughing.

"I wonder how that guy who bought the Vyrus is doing," said one.

"Ten to one it's been repo'd," said the other.

"Yeah, that guy had no business buying that gorgeous machine. Not only could he not afford it—he couldn't ride worth beans."

The first salesman shook his head, "I guess as long as he thought he had the money, it was our job to sell him the most expensive machine on the lot."

They continued laughing, and the vision faded.

"No—wait!" cried Ike, "Does it have to be that way? Will Penny be left penniless? Wait, that makes no sense— if she is Penny she could never be penniless. Well anyway, spirit, you know what I mean."

The coin said nothing. Ike only saw Susan B. Anthony's steely stare (ironic, since the Susan B. Anthony dollar is made of copper-nickel clad).

"Is it too late? I'll change (another ironic statement, since Ike was talking to a coin), I'll pay my debts, I won't overspend! Tell me what I've seen doesn't have to be!

With a poof, the coin vanished. Ike was alone.

Ike wasn't actually alone; Penny had been in bed, sound asleep the entire time. Ike couldn't help but wonder how Penny could sleep through all the racket yet still complain about his snoring. That, however, was a subject for another day.

Ike awoke after a fitful sleep. He could almost recall the images he saw in his dreams but the more he tried to remember, the more elusive they became until finally, they were gone.

A feeling remained, however. That feeling was the conviction he and Penny had to get out of debt. Now that he knew the interest on their credit cards was something they paid, not something they received, he was determined to eliminate that liability as soon as possible. Ike knew he had to make some changes, and fast.

The next morning, he would call Mae's office to schedule another appointment, but this time with a different attitude.

Chapter 10
Repairing the Damage
Getting out of Debt and Staying Out of Debt

"Wake up!" Ike exclaimed, snapping the elastic on Penny's sleep mask.

Fortunately for Ike, Penny was a sound-sleeper and awoke unaware of the red stripe gradually appearing on the side of her face.

Truth be told, Penny was relieved Ike was paying any attention to her at all. For the past few years he'd spent more time in the garage than the house.

"What is it?" Penny asked.

"I'm a changed man," said Ike, "I've had a dream—an epiphany! Not only do I want to get out of debt and spend less, I may even want kids."

Penny was dumbfounded. She was also a bit skeptical. She knew she must quickly take advantage of this window of opportunity.

Looking into his eyes and trying to determine his sincerity, she asked, "Can we go back to Lotta Branes for more financial counseling?"

"Sure," said Ike, "and on the way home, maybe we can stop by Babies R Us. You never know what might be in store for our family in the near future."

Penny was ecstatic! She had always been excited at the prospect of having a baby. Or two. Or nine.

On the way to Lotta's office, Ike obeyed the speed limit. "Wow," thought Penny, "Ike really is different!"

Lotta smiled when she saw Ike and Penny arriving in the same car. "That's a good sign," she thought to herself.

Once seated in Lotta's office, they began examining the details of their credit card problem.

The $40,000 of debt was divided among 4 bank cards and 3 retail-store cards. $10,000 was owed to a VISA card issued by Mammoth Bank with an annual interest-rate of 28.99%. $7,000 was owed to another VISA card from Big Metropolis Trust at a rate of 22.9%. Their MasterCard came from Huge Vaults Savings and Loan, and carried a 15.99% interest rate on $6,000. The remaining bank card carried a balance of $5,000 at 11.99% and was issued by Das Grossbank.

The retail credit cards totaled $12,000: Tool Emporium--$4,000 at 24.99%; The Kitchen Clutter Store--$5,000 at 19.99%; and Man-Cave Supply--$3,000 at 12.99%.

Lotta explained there are two main philosophies when it comes to paying down debt.

The first is to make minimum payments to all debts except the one with the lowest balance. All available funds in excess of payments to the larger debts are used to pay the smallest debt. Once that debt is retired, its payment is added to the payment of the next-largest debt until it is paid off, then those payments are combined and paid toward the next-largest, and so on, until all debts are gone.

The other approach is to use the same tactic, except instead of first paying off the smallest debt, the balance with the highest interest rate is made the priority. Once that debt is gone, extra payments are made to the debt with the next highest rate, etc.

Although the latter may make more sense from a pure financial standpoint, the former is often more successful. The emotional satisfaction of cutting up a newly-paid-off credit card in a short amount of time can be inspiring, even if it only had a small balance and a low interest rate. Starting with a high-interest card with a large balance may seem overwhelming.

Before doing anything, though, Lotta recommended Ike and Penny call their existing banks to ask if any of them offered a balance transfer program which would help them consolidate their cards at a lower interest rate.

"In fact," Lotta told them, "you might not have to transfer anything because sometimes banks will lower their interest rates if you just ask. If balance transfers are your only option, you may incur a balance-transfer fee, but a lower overall interest-rate on the total debt could mitigate that in a fairly short time."

Penny remembered the last time she tried calling the bank. After being put on hold for 20 minutes, repeatedly pushing buttons so the reassuring robot-voice could know her name, age, account number, Social Security number, address, phone number, mother's maiden name, PIN, user name, password, first stuffed animal, city in which she was born, and eye color, she was put on hold for another 20 minutes. Finally, she was transferred to someone who spoke in a language so foreign that it was difficult for Penny to tell she was being asked the exact same questions she had just answered with her myriad button-pushing.

Still, if going through that again could lower their interest rate...

"With this new debt-reduction regime, will I still be able to continue my subscription to 'Fast Bikes and the Men Who Love Them'?" asked Ike.

"It depends," answered Lotta, "you're going to need a budget. I think you need an in-and-out account."

Hearing the term "in-and-out" reminded Ike of hamburgers, and suddenly he felt hungry.

"The way it works," continued Lotta, "is we design a chart with columns representing all your monthly expenditures. Expenses that occur semi-annually, annually, or at other intervals are divided and spread out over each month. Every time you get a paycheck, the money you receive is allocated to each column. That means for every expense category, you know exactly how much is available to spend each month. For example, if you have $125 allocated to dining out and during the first week of the month you spend $100 at McDonalds, this means you only have $25 remaining for dining out that month."

Although Ike had been truly changed by his epiphanous dream, he was still subject to Maslow's hierarchy of needs. All this talk of food was hampering his ability to concentrate on budget charts.

"Ike!" Penny exclaimed, "pay attention!"

Ike snapped out of his stupor.

"Sorry—I really was trying to pay attention."

"It's Ok," Lotta reassured him, "this stuff can seem boring. Once you get in the habit of paying your bills this way, though, you'll see how helpful it is. Some people even use separate envelopes, labeling them for different categories and literally put cash in each one on payday. When the envelope is empty, no more money can be spent in that area until the next payday."

"So," Penny mused, "even though we pay our insurance every six months, as long as we were putting the right amount in the 'car insurance' envelope every month, when the bill comes due we'd have enough."

"Exactly," replied Lotta, "and the same is true for clothing, gifts, and all your other expenses."

"Couldn't we just create a spreadsheet on our computer to handle this?" asked Ike.

Penny was stunned—Ike was actually getting this!

"Sure," said Lotta, "In fact, that's a great idea."

"I don't know if our current computer is up to the task," Penny pointed out. "It's pretty old."

"Yes," added Ike, "it's my Commodore Amiga 1000 from college. Doesn't the fact it has the number 1000 in its name mean it's futuristic and cool?"

"As cool as the parachute pants hanging in your closet," laughed Penny, "and just about as useful!"

Lotta interrupted, "It seems to me you need to write 'new computer' on one of your envelopes."

Ike and Penny nodded in agreement. "If you have smart phones, there are even apps you can download which do most of the work for you. Your mission, should you choose to accept it, is to design your personal in-and-out account spreadsheet, and don't forget to include an investment category. Even though your main focus is getting out of debt, we need to make sure you're saving for the future, too."

"We don't know a lot about investments," admitted Penny.

"But we're willing to learn," added Ike.

"Great," Lotta replied, "the next time we meet, I'll review your budgeting and explain some of the basics of investing."

Ike and Penny left Lotta's office feeling more encouraged than they had in years.

Chapter 11
SHOULD YOU BUY MOTORCYCLES, SHELBY COBRAS, AND AMC PACERS?
BASICS OF INVESTING

Ike and Penny worked together to build the in-and-out account recommended by Lotta. Ike commented it was a lotta hard work and took levels of concentration he hadn't experienced in...actually, Ike had never experienced that level of concentration.

They finally finished listing all their expenses, each divided into monthly increments. To Ike and Penny, the column marked "investments" was still a mystery. Any extra money Ike earned had been invested in a portfolio of motorcycles--not the greatest retirement-funding vehicle, but as far as Ike was concerned, the best vehicles for him.

Time for another visit to Lotta to find out what investments might be more appropriate than motorcycles, albeit less exciting.

"There are many ways to invest," Lotta began, "but the idea is to own something which, over time, increases in value so when sold at a future date you realize a profit."

"If you buy something, oh, say, like a motorcycle," asked Penny, "and it drops in value by half, what kind of investment is that?"

Before Lotta could say a word, Ike piped up, "A fun one!"

"Actually," Lotta replied, "in some cases a loss in one investment could be used against a gain in another investment. That could be helpful in lowering your taxes."

"So taxes and investments are connected?" asked Penny.

"Yep," said Lotta, "but that's a subject for another meeting—and it can get really complicated. For now, let's just stick to the basics."

Ike felt his eyelids getting heavy.

Lotta noticed, "To continue, let's say in 1966 you bought a Shelby Cobra."

Ike perked right up.

"At that time, the cost was about six-thousand dollars which was a lot of money back then. Today, an original Shelby Cobra Super Snake might sell for as much as five million dollars."

Being a true car-guy, Ike began to feel smug.

"How much money," Lotta continued, "have you made on your investment?"

Penny answered, "Four million, nine-hundred nine-ty-four thousand dollars."

Lotta smiled, "Yes and no. First of all, if you haven't sold it, you haven't made anything. You only make money when someone hands you the cash and takes the title. Remember I said I wasn't going to talk about taxes? In this case, it's very relevant. Because the value increased by so much, you might have to pay close to two million dollars to Uncle Sam. It depends on a lot of factors, but let's assume you ended up with three million dollars, after taxes. That's about thirteen and a half percent per year of growth on your initial, six-thou-sand-dollar investment, which is amazing."

Now Ike was feeling really smug.

"But there aren't a lot of things that end up being worth that much!" Penny protested.

"That's right, agreed Lotta, plus, if it rusted away to nothing, you could lose your entire investment."

"Aluminum doesn't rust," Ike sniffed.

"That's not the point," Penny shot back, "what if I bought an AMC Pacer? Those things are almost worthless."

"Actually," Lott pointed out, "they used to be almost worthless, and if you sold one ten years ago you would have certainly lost money. If, however, you had held onto it and kept it in tip-top shape, you might be able to sell it now and actually make a profit! The key is not selling at the wrong time."

Lotta continued, "Anyway, the point is when it comes to investing, diversification is good. Diversification is really nothing more than taking your grandma's advice: Don't put all your eggs in one basket."

Ike thought for a moment, "In other words, I should buy motorcycles and a Cobra."

"Well, you've got the right idea," Lotta chuckled, "but having two kinds of motorized vehicles isn't too diversified."

Penny's eyes lit up, "So what you're saying is, it would make more sense to buy some motorcycles, some cars, some sewing machines, some furniture, some kitchen appliances…"

Ike interrupted, "Some tools, some lawn mowers, some guns, some bowling balls…"

"Exactly," said Lotta, "but do you see the problem? It would take a lot of money to buy enough items to really be diversified. For example, even if you had all those items stashed in your garage, if a tree fell and demolished it all, your entire investment would be gone. You'd need items stored in garages all over the country to minimize your risk; maybe even all over the world."

"How do people like us invest in so many different things?" asked Penny, "we don't have that kind of money or that many garages to possibly diversify enough."

"I've got good news for you. There is a way, and we'll talk about it during our next visit. We'll look at mutual funds, and how they might be just what you need."

"So you'll put the fun in mutual funds?" Ike chortled.

"Um, yeah," replied Lotta.

Penny rolled her eyes.

Chapter 12
THE FEELING IS MUTUAL
MUTUAL FUNDS

When I.M. Rich and Penny Pincher got married, neither knew in just a few short years they'd be talking to a financial planner about investing. Not only was their financial planner, Lotta Branes, one smart cookie, she also excelled in the art of persuasion. The fact she had persuaded Ike to channel some of his income away from motorcycles and into investments was nothing short of miraculous.

"So," Ike began, "you were going to tell us about mutual funds. I've heard of those before—one of my buddies at work is always bragging about how smart he is at picking the right mutual funds and making money."

"Sure," Lotta laughed, "and I bet he always wins in Vegas, too."

"Come to think of it, not so much..." Ike's voice trailed off.

"There are many ways to invest, but since most people are invested in mutual funds, usually in their 401(k) plans or individual retirement accounts, we'll start there. Mutual funds, like any investment, have some risk. Different mutual funds have different levels of risk depending on all kinds of factors. Before we get into that, though, let me give you some basics on what a mutual fund actually is."

Ike furrowed his brow and Penny leaned forward.

"The technical definition is," Lotta continued, "a mutual fund is an open-ended investment company which pools people's money."

Ike furrowed his brow even further,

"What's an open-ended investment company?" Penny asked.

"Open-ended means its shares can be traded on an exchange. It's an investment company because its purpose is to invest its shareholder's money. That money comes from many different people so they are pooling their resources."

By this time Ike's brow looked like a pretzel. "Wait, wait, wait," he protested, "shares? Traded on an exchange? Shareholder? What are you talking about?"

Penny winced, but Lotta was nothing if not patient, so she continued.

"Think of it this way, Ike: Suppose I wanted to start my own mutual fund. I'll call it the 'Lotta Fun Fund' and I want to invest in toy companies. In order to invest in multiple toy companies, I'll need a lot of money. Let's say you and a bunch of your friends also want to invest in toy companies but none of you has enough money to invest in more than one or two. Since your mom always told you not to put all your eggs in one basket, you aren't happy investing in only a couple of toy companies. After all, what if one of them turns out to be the next F.A.O. Schwarz? Instead, you decide to get together with your friends and pool your money. That's where the Lotta Fun Fund comes in. Rather than you and your friends trying to buy dozens or even hundreds of shares of different toy stores, you each buy a share of my new investment company—the Lotta Fun mutual fund. I take a little money off the top as my fee and then invest the rest in all sorts of toy stores. That fee, by the way, is part of the fund's expense ratio. There are other costs inside of mutual funds, too, which you need to be aware of before you invest. If the toy stores in which I invest grow in value, so does the value of my mutual fund. You own a share--a small piece--of my mutual fund, so your share goes up in value."

Ike's brow was unfurrowing. "What if you invest in a bunch of dumb toy stores that don't do well or go out of business?"

"What do you think would happen?" asked Lotta.

"I suppose I'd lose money."

"Not exactly. You'd only lose money if you sold your share to someone else for less than you paid for it. Likewise, you haven't made any money unless you sell the share for more than you paid for it. Until then, it's only a paper gain or loss; what we call an unrealized gain or an unrealized loss. Of course, it's more complicated than that because mutual funds are required to pass on to the mutual fund shareholders taxes for each transaction, so one mutual fund may have many realized and unrealized gains and losses tied to the various stocks, bonds, or other investments it holds. "

Ike beamed. "I realize I know what you mean!"

Lotta turned to Penny, "Are you following all this?"

"I think so, but I've heard of something called an index fund. What's that?"

"Great question! By asking that you're opening up a financial-planning can of worms that has been debated for as long as there have been investments. It has to do with investment philosophy: Active versus passive."

"Hey, that describes us!" exclaimed Ike, "I'm the passive one."

"Right," chuckled Penny, "and if you believe that, I have a bridge you can buy."

By now Lotta wasn't paying much attention to Ike--or Penny, for that matter--she was too excited about delving into such a controversial subject.

"You see, if in the mutual fund example I gave a minute ago I was buying and selling toy store stocks using my knowledge and expertise to do the right thing at the right time, the fund would be considered actively managed. On the other hand, if I just bought a certain group of toy stores, say the largest 100 toy stores in the country, and then simply held them in my fund without making any changes, my fund could be considered a passive investment. If the 100 toy stores were a recognized representation of a certain segment of toy stores, those stores might be called a 'toy store index." If that were the case, my mutual fund would be called an index fund. Since I wouldn't have to make day-to-day buying and selling decisions, my fee could be much less than it would be in an active mutual fund."

Penny was curious. "Which is better? Investing in the least-expensive index fund, or paying for active management?"

Lotta shook her head. "I'm going to give you the same answer I always get whenever I ask the IRS a question: 'It depends.' In most cases, over the long-term, index funds have achieved higher returns than their actively-managed counterparts, but that's not always true. Sometimes, good managers can outperform the index, or come close but with less volatility."

"Volatility?" asked Ike.

"Yes," said Lotta, "that's how far up and down the value of an investment goes during a given time period. The technical term is standard deviation. In many cases an actively-managed fund can have less volatility than an index, since if things start to tank, the manager can sell certain positions to help stop the bleeding."

"Do mutual funds always invest in stocks?" inquired Penny.

"Not at all!" exclaimed Lotta, who was still giddy with excitement because she loved talking about the technical side of investing. "They can invest in bonds, short-term money-market instruments, even options or other esoteric securities and investments. The key for most mutual-fund investors is to build a portfolio of mutual funds with different objectives, so if one fund is investing in things that aren't doing well, another fund might be experiencing growth. That's called diversifying."

"So," Ike piped up, "when it comes to investing, we're going to need some diversity training!"

"It couldn't hurt."

"Is there anything else we should know about mutual funds?" asked Penny.

"There's a lot more," said Lotta, "much more than we can cover now. But let me tell you about one other aspect of mutual funds, before you go. This has to do with what's known as a fund's share class."

"Frankly," said Ike, "I would never use the words 'Cher' and 'class' in the same sentence."

"No, no," Lotta was a bit exasperated, "it's 'share' not 'Cher…'"

Penny rolled her eyes which were getting tired from all the rolling.

"Share class describes how certain sales charges and fees are assessed on mutual fund purchases. For example, A-share mutual funds usually charge an up-front commission of up to 5.5% or more. When a certain amount is invested in one fund or fund family within a certain time, the buyer might reach what are called 'break points.' The sales charge usually gets reduced at these pre-determined levels. The maximum sales load allowed by the regulatory agency FINRA is a whopping 8.5%, but almost no fund charges that much."

"FINRA sounds like something that should regulate the fishing industry," laughed Ike.

Ignoring him (something Penny had learned to do years ago), Lotta continued, "B-share mutual funds don't charge an up-front fee, but instead subject the investor to what are called 'deferred sales charges' which decline over time."

Ike's brow furrowed again. The only time he had heard the word "deferred" was when he was in court.

"The way it works," Lotta explained, "is if you were to invest in a B-share mutual fund but then decided you wanted to take some or all of your money out, if you did so during the first year, the mutual fund company would keep 5% of the money. If you took money out during the second year, they'd keep 4%, and so on, until the fifth or sixth year when there would no longer be any more deferred sales charges, at least on the original purchase."

"Wouldn't that make them better than A-share funds, since if you don't take money out for a while there's no sales charge, like with an A share?" asked Penny

"Well," said Lotta, "that would be true except that B-share funds usually have higher internal fees than A-share funds, so over time owning a B-share could actually cost the investor more than the A-share version of the same fund."

"I see."

"Speaking of C, that's another share-class of mutual funds. C-share funds usually have a small initial sales charge, a shorter deferred sales charge period, but also have higher internal fees than A-share funds. They can be useful for someone who wants to invest in a mutual fund for a limited period of time. Of course, anytime anyone talks about investing for a limited amount of time, it raises the hair on the back of my neck."

Ike tried not to think about Lotta's neck hair.

"I remember hearing investing isn't a short-term proposition--is that right?" asked Penny.

"Absolutely! I think it was none other than Warren Buffet who said there is no such thing as short-term investing—that's called speculating. There are other share classes of mutual funds used in retirement accounts or for larger investments, but we don't have time to cover all of the different share classes now."

"That's OK," said Ike, "you've shared so much already. Penny and I really appreciate you sharing all this information. As we always say, 'share and share alike.'"

Penny sighed (while rolling her eyes yet again), "Come on, Ike, let's go, I bet Lotta's got a lotta things to do."

"One last thing," asked Ike, "what if Penny is concerned about the volatility of mutual funds? Is there some kind of investment that offers some guarantees? I really want to be sure Penny feels secure."

"There is," Lotta assured him. "Often, people who want guarantees look to annuities. They can be very complicated, so let's dedicate the next few sessions to discussing them."

Penny missed Lotta's last comment because she was so shocked Ike would consider her need for security. "Yes," she thought, "all this talk of investing and planning really is helping Ike mature."

Her daydreaming abruptly ground to a halt as they left and Ike began running down the up escalator while making car sounds.

Chapter 13
THE FIX(ED) IS IN
ANNUITY BASICS

Ike and Penny were filled with trepidation. Today, they were on their way to the office of Lotta Branes, their financial advisor, to discuss annuities.

Ike and Penny had heard that annuities were terrible--almost satanic.

They had also heard they were wonderful--almost miraculous.

Ike had heard annuities had high fees, illiquidity, poor investment options, terrible estate-planning attributes, and potential tax-penalties.

Penny had heard annuities provided guarantees, income which couldn't be outlived, a myriad of investment options, death-benefits for heirs, principal safety, and tax deferral.

Although Ike and Penny had different opinions concerning annuities, they had never actually argued about them. Their disagreements mainly centered around such pressing issues as whether they should buy a new dishwasher or replace Ike's old Kenwood receiver with a Goldmund Epilogue Signature audio system.

The audio system remained low on the priority list.

They arrived at Lotta's office, made themselves comfortable, and Lotta began.

"Annuities are interesting. They kind of remind me of the Government. Originally, the Government was relatively simple and easy to understand. Over the years, however, it has gotten more complicated and confusing with so many pages of rules and regulations it would take several lifetimes to read them all."

"How much can you cover in an hour?" Ike grumbled, "that's about all the time we have."

Lotta sighed. "In that case, for now we'll just stick to the basics. I'll talk about fixed annuities, immediate annuities, deferred annuities and their payout options. We'll save variable annuities and equity-indexed annuities for future visits."

"Wonderful," Ike groaned. He was genuinely interested in providing security for Penny, but only if it didn't interfere with Gilligan's Island at 4 PM.

"Go on," Penny urged, "We've heard so much conflicting information about annuities I can't wait to get the straight scoop."

Ike's thoughts drifted to chocolate ice cream.

"OK," Lotta began, "the original concept of an annuity is a guaranteed stream of income provided from a person or entity to another person or entity."

"You mean like my dad's pension?" asked Penny.

"Yes," Lotta replied, "a pension can be considered a type of annuity payment. Usually, though, an annuity is offered by an insurance company. The insurance company offers guaranteed payments in exchange for a chunk of money. You give the company a lump sum; they give you payments. The most basic annuity is the immediate, life-only annuity. In this arrangement, the insurance company is given an amount of money, and based on the life expectancy of the annuitant, payments are made until the annuitant dies. Once the payments begin, we say the annuity has been 'annuitized' and the money is under the control of the insurance company. It's been converted into a stream of income and the annuitant can't get back the lump sum. It now belongs to the insurance company."

"Annuitant?" scoffed Ike, "what's with the goofy name?"

"It's not goofy," scolded Penny, "that's one of those fancy, financial words."

Lotta continued, "In an annuity contract, there are up to 4 parties involved."

Ike perked up—he liked parties.

"The four parties are the issuer of the annuity, the owner, the annuitant, and the beneficiary. As I mentioned earlier, the issuer is usually an insurance company, but this isn't always the case. Sometimes a charitable organization can offer annuity payments to donors, and even individuals could set up an annuity contract if they wanted.

The owner is the person who requested the annuity in the first place. He or she can decide who gets the payout, how long the payout lasts, and other aspects of the contract.

The annuitant is on whose life expectancy the payments are based. Often, the owner and annuitant are the same person.

The beneficiary is the person who receives any remaining benefit or payments after the owner dies. In a life-only annuity, however, there wouldn't be anything left over after the owner dies, because when that happens the payments stop."

"Wait just a second!" Ike protested, "you mean if I give a million dollars to an insurance company, start my annuity payments and then die a week later the million dollars is, 'poof,' just gone?"

"It's not really gone," explained Lotta, "the insurance company got it."

"That's what I mean!" exclaimed Ike, "I don't have it—I'm dead. Penny doesn't have it, even if she stays alive—it all went to the insurance company. What a rip-off."

"Keep your hair on." Penny sounded exasperated. "Just think what would happen if you lived to be 100. The insurance company would be on the hook for all those payments."

"If the annuitant were very old when the annuity was purchased," Lotta added, "the guaranteed payments would have to be really big, or it wouldn't be worth doing. The owner hopes he or she will last a long time and receive more money back than what was given to the insurance company. The insurance company hopes, well, I don't know if we can say the insurance company hopes the client will die soon, but it sure doesn't hurt the bottom line if that's what happens."

"Kinda morbid," Penny mused.

"If you look at it that way, I guess it is," Lotta continued, "On the other hand, if you want to be sure you're never going to run out of income, a life annuity can be quite reassuring.

Ike relaxed a bit, "I suppose. But what if I wanted someone to keep getting the payments after I croaked? Is there an annuity that does that?"

"Yes," Lotta answered, "insurance companies have come up with some options to help mitigate the concern of an annuitant dying too soon. One is what's called a joint-and-survivor annuity. It pays until the second of two people dies."

The fact an annuity could have something to do with a joint intrigued Ike almost as much as reruns of Gilligan's Island.

Lotta went on, "In fact, you can even set up an annuity to pay for the longer of someone's life or a certain number of years. That's called a life-with-period-certain annuity."

Penny felt as if a light bulb was going off inside her head. "So, if we wanted to, we could buy a joint-and-survivor, 10-year certain annuity which would pay Ike and me until the last one of us died, even if one of us lived to 110, but if we were both killed in a car accident 3 years after starting the annuity, our kids would keep getting payments for another 7 years?"

"Assuming the insurance company remained solvent that is correct."

"I think I get it!" Penny said, triumphantly.

"What about you, Ike?" Lotta asked.

"I think so. But what if I don't want to start getting payments right away?"

"In that case, you could purchase a deferred annuity. A deferred annuity does exactly what its name implies. You give the money to the insurance company, but the payments are deferred until a later date."

"If the insurance company gets to keep my money for a while before starting to give it back, how does that help me?" Ike inquired.

"Usually the insurance company pays interest on the money it holds in an annuity. In a fixed annuity, the interest rate can vary from time to time, but usually has a minimum guaranteed amount below which the rate will never go. Years ago, you might be able to get a floor of four percent or more. Now, not so much—maybe you'll get a one-percent minimum."

"Couldn't I just invest the money myself and make more?" asked Ike.

"Perhaps, but remember, fixed annuities are guaranteed by the insurance company. Other types of investments may have the potential for higher gains, but usually carry higher risk. You raise a good point though. One of the advantages of annuities is tax-deferral. If you take out annuity earnings before age 59 ½ there's a penalty, but if you can wait until after that, the fact you don't pay tax on the growth until you begin distributions can help the annuity grow more quickly than a taxable investment might. Insurance companies realized this could be especially powerful if the annuity principal could be invested in securities, which do have the potential for significant growth. Thus, the variable annuity was born.

We'll talk about that during our next meeting."

Wait," Penny said, "You said there's a penalty for taking money from an annuity?"

"There are exceptions. For example, if you annuitize an annuity, the 10% penalty generally doesn't apply. Also, in the event of death or disability the penalty may not apply. There are other exceptions, too, but those are questions for the insurance company and your CPA."

"Thanks so much for explaining all this," Ike said, checking his watch, "I can't wait until we get to see you a Gilligan…I mean, again."

Penny rolled her eyes.

Chapter 14
IT'S COMPLICATED...
VARIABLE ANNUITIES

During their last visit with Lotta, Ike and Penny learned about the somewhat confusing world of fixed annuities. They arrived once again, hoping to begin unraveling the massively complicated, obfuscating, bewildering, mystifying, flummoxing, vexing, mind-numbing, exasperating, baffling, befuddling, confounding, disorienting, frustrating, muddling, perplexing, puzzling, unsettling world of variable annuities.

Ike was feeling good, since after Lotta had explained the ins-and-outs of fixed annuities, he had actually understood what she said. Better yet, Penny understood too. This meant if Ike only thought he understood, Penny could retrain him. Best of all, last week's appointment with Lotta ended in time for Ike to get home and watch not only Gilligan's Island, but The Munsters, too.

Ike and Penny made their way up the stairs and into Lotta's office.

Penny walked, but Ike's confidence in his newfound financial wisdom elevated him from walking to striding.

As they got comfortable around the table and Ike rifled through the candy dish, Penny noticed that Lotta looked concerned.

"Is everything alright?" Penny asked.

Ike noticed, too, and wondered if he should have only taken 3 peanut butter cups.

"Oh, I'm fine," reassured Lotta, "it's just that our subject today can be very confusing—almost overwhelming. There's so much to cover."

"Great!" Ike thought, "I'll never get home in time to watch Gilligan's Island, and I might miss Bewitched, too."

"We should get started right away," Penny suggested.

Lotta summarized their last meeting's discussion about fixed annuities. "Do you remember just before you left I mentioned using variable investments inside of an annuity?"

"Yes," replied Penny.

Ike just nodded (his mouth was full of peanut butter cups).

"OK, let's begin there. During times when the stock market is going up, fixed annuities don't seem particularly exciting to investors since the interest-rates on fixed annuities can be pretty conservative. This is one of the reasons insurance companies which can offer security-based products decided to offer variable annuities. If the money inside the annuity is in what we call 'variable investments' such as stock and bond portfolios, there can be a potential for the annuity to grow in value more quickly than a fixed annuity would. Plus, you still have the benefit of tax-deferred growth."

"That sounds nice," Penny said.

"What's the catch?" Ike asked, through the last bite of peanut butter cup.

"Well, along with the potential advantages there are some disadvantages. For example, if the markets stink, you could end up with less value than the initial premium payment. Also, there are several layers of fees. Granted, there are fees in fixed annuities, too, but they are built into the product so you don't readily see them. In a variable annuity, most fees are individually broken out and visible. They're listed in the prospectus."

"Listed in the prospectus? Visible?" Ike scoffed, "The last time I tried reading one of those dumb prospectuses I couldn't make heads or tails out of it."

"It's true," Lotta agreed, "over the years prospectuses have gotten longer and more complicated, but for a basic, variable annuity, there are certain, typical fees. First, the mortality and expense fee. This can be less than 1%, but is usually in the 1.25% range. You see, most annuities offer some kind of death-benefit guarantee. If you put a certain amount of money in an annuity and then die before using up its value, the insurance company can provide the beneficiaries with the greater of what is actually in the annuity when you die, or if investment performance has been poor, the total premium payments less withdrawals. That's some of what the mortality and expense fee covers."

Ike was skeptical. "You mean if I put a million dollars in a variable annuity, the market crashes dropping its value to $500,000, I open the latest statement and because it's lost so much money I die of a heart attack, Penny would still get a cool million?"

"That's the idea. The mortality and expense fee also covers things such as commissions, and selling and administrative expenses. There are other fees, too, though. For instance, the investments within a variable annuity have a management fee. This fee pays the person or team who makes the investment decisions in each subaccount, and in some cases, can also cover marketing expenses and other internal costs."

"I wonder if any of the subaccounts ever go nuclear…" (Ike was cracking himself up). "It sure would be a shame if a subaccount torpedoed an investment! Do any subaccounts ever take a dive?"

Lotta paid no attention and continued. "There are other fees which can be assessed in a variable annuity, depending on what additional riders the owner may want to include."

"Like Riders on the Storm?" Ike offered. (He loved the Doors.)

Penny elbowed him.

"For instance," Lotta said, ignoring Ike's nonsense, "some variable annuities offer an enhanced death benefit. This could mean the beneficiary gets more than the original premium payment either through periodic step-ups, death proceeds based on the annuity's highest value at some point in time, or other formulas an insurance company includes in its available riders. The company might offer some sort of return of premium, so that even if the annuity's investments do badly, the owner can get back everything he or she paid into the annuity at some future time. There may be some sort of bonus which adds to the annuity value if you don't take withdrawals and keep the annuity in force for a prescribed number of years. A bonus like that might only be accessible if you annuitize the annuity. All these kinds of options are additional riders which add additional cost."

Lotta took a deep breath, "and then there's what's known as 'living benefits.'"

"Living benefits?" Penny wrinkled her nose.

Ike remembered he was missing Bewitched.

"This is where things get really complicated," Lotta admitted. "Even though some of the features I mentioned earlier could be considered living benefits because they can be an advantage to the annuity owner when he or she is still alive, the living benefits I'm referring to now have to do with income payments. There's no way I can explain all the different iterations in the time we have left. The best I can do today is give you an overview. If you ever consider buying a variable annuity, I suggest you bring me the prospectus and marketing materials so I can review it before you make any decisions. Let's continue--there is still a lot to cover."

Ike began to realize there would be no Munsters tonight, either.

"Remember what we talked about last time: One of the disadvantages of annuitizing a traditional annuity is once you make the election to annuitize, you give control of the assets to the insurance company. In other words, in the old days, once you began receiving guaranteed payments you lost access to the principal. Somewhere along the way someone had the bright idea to offer guaranteed payments without the requirement to annuitize the contract. The thought was, someone could buy an annuity, start receiving periodic payments, but still have access to the principal if life circumstances changed. Also, in the event the owner died, his or her beneficiaries could receive whatever was left in the annuity as a lump sum rather than having to receive payments, or worse, have it go to the insurance company."

"That sounds pretty good," Penny said.

"That sounds pretty expensive," Ike said.

"You're both correct. That feature can be a very good thing for the right person, but it does cost money. Usually, a rider like that can add another percent or more to the cost of a variable annuity. There is something more, though, I haven't told you yet. The payments may not be based solely on the annuity's current investment value. Some companies track the performance of the investments and periodically record the value for income purposes. This can be calculated daily, monthly, or in some cases yearly. That value is 'locked-in,' as it were, and when it comes time to begin taking distributions, some percentage of that number or the actual value of the annuity at that time, whichever is greater, is used to determine the payout rate. The payout rate is usually around 4 to 6 percent, maybe a bit higher or lower depending on the particular insurance company and the annuitant's age—or ages if the annuity has a spousal feature. Some companies even provide an assumed growth rate they apply, so even if the investments don't grow, the amount on which the future income stream is based does increase. Of course, the amount on which the payments are based isn't necessarily what the annuity is worth if surrendered for a lump-sum—it's simply an income-base."

Ike felt his head beginning to get light. "That sounds expensive and confusing," he mumbled. "In fact," he looked at the ceiling for a moment, deep in thought, "if I am adding up the numbers correctly, a person could be paying north of 3% in fees for one of these annuities with living benefits, right?"

"That's true," replied Lotta, "but let me ask you something. What are Volvos known for? Speed? Stunning good looks?"

If there was one subject Ike knew, it was cars, "No!" he stated, emphatically, "they're known for safety."

"And they aren't the cheapest cars on the road, are they?"

"No."

"So, if they aren't the fastest cars on the road, and they aren't the most beautiful, why would people pay more for them?"

"Because they're safe." (Ike knew Penny had always wanted a Volvo--now he knew why.)

"Exactly! And just like the fact not everyone cares about safety and therefore won't pay the higher price for a Volvo, not everyone chooses to pay variable annuity fees in exchange for the corresponding guarantees—or safety, if you will. For some people, though, the ability to invest in various portfolios while still having a guaranteed, predictable, future stream of income from the insurance company is worth the extra cost."

"Hmm," this made sense to Ike, "but what kind of formulas are used to figure out the guaranteed payouts? You mentioned locking in the annuity's value at certain times-- how does that work? And are there other disadvantages we should know about?"

"As I said earlier, each insurance company has its own variation on the theme, and some are so complicated even I struggle to comprehend them. My advice is this: After talking with an adviser and having him or her answer all your questions, if you still don't understand the product, don't buy it. As far as other disadvantages, there are a few. For example, even though you get tax-deferred earnings in an annuity, when you take distributions of the money which hasn't been taxed while it was growing in the annuity, they are generally taxed at ordinary-income rates, which might be higher than capital-gains rates available if you invested in a standard, taxable, brokerage account. Also, most annuities have surrender charges."

Ike's thoughts immediately switched to his favorite science-fiction movie and he blurted out, "Never give up! Never surrender..." his voice trailed off as he realized neither Lotta nor Penny had seen Galaxy Quest and didn't know what he was talking about.

"Anyway," Lotta continued, slightly annoyed, "we talked about this before. Surrender charges are penalties levied against an annuity owner who takes distributions too soon after buying an annuity. They differ in amount and in how long they last, depending on the specific annuity. A typical surrender charge schedule might be 7 years, with a penalty of 8% in each of the first three years, 7% in the fourth year, 6% in the fifth year, 5% in the sixth year, and 4% in the seventh year. After the seventh year, the insurance company would release all the funds to the owner if the owner wanted them. Often, the insurance company will allow a certain amount to be taken out each year before the surrender charges kick in, but the fact most annuities have some sort of surrender charges illustrates that annuities are generally thought to be long-term investments, not something you'd start one year and surrender the next. For example, if at age 60 you bought a $100,000 annuity like the one I just described and decided to take your money out during the first year, assuming the company allowed a 10% free withdrawal, you'd leave 8% of $90,000 with the insurance company—that's $7,200. As I pointed out last week, usually the surrender charges don't apply if the owner dies or becomes disabled, though. Oh yes, and if you take earnings out of an annuity before 59 1/2, unless you qualify for one of the few exceptions, you'll pay a 10% IRS penalty in addition to the normal taxes due."

"That is a lot to remember," Penny sighed.

"Yes," replied Lotta, "and that's not even covering all you need to know about variable annuities. You really need to read each prospectus and talk about it with me or another qualified financial adviser. Variable annuities are complex and not for everybody, but for the right person they can offer a good balance of growth potential, protection, and security."

"Next time you come in," Lotta continued, "We'll talk about another kind of annuity—equity-indexed annuities."

"Are they more like fixed annuities or variable annuities?" asked Ike.

"Yes," Lotta smiled, "and we'll talk about that next time you're here."

Chapter 15
WAIT, IT'S EVEN MORE COMPLICATED!
EQUITY-INDEXED ANNUITIES

Ike and Penny had talked with Lotta Branes, their financial adviser about the massively complicated, obfuscating, bewildering, mystifying, flummoxing, vexing, mind-numbing, exasperating, baffling, befuddling, confounding, disorienting, frustrating, muddling, perplexing, puzzling, unsettling world of variable annuities. They were about to leave for their next appointment, wondering if the same adjectives could be applied to equity-indexed annuities, too.

Penny was anxious to leave for the appointment, but she found it difficult to tear Ike way from his computer. He was deeply involved with friends from around the world in a game of League of Legends.

"Ike! Ike!" she pleaded, "come on, we've got to go—we have a lotta things to talk about with Lotta."

Even Penny's wit wasn't enough to break his concentration. Finally, in desperation, Penny yanked the power cord from the wall.

The computer went dead and Ike came alive.

"What are you doing?" he protested, "I had a lot of time invested in that game!"

"I'm glad you're interested in investments, because we have an appointment with Lotta to discuss that very issue."

Ike scowled. He had completely forgotten about the meeting.

"Alright," he said, "I guess Darius can wait."

"Who?"

"Never mind." Ike never understood how Penny could be so concerned with their future when she could be enjoying video games instead.

As they arrived at her office, Lotta welcomed them and took them to the conference room.

"At our last meeting," she began, "we talked about a rather complicated subject—variable annuities. Well, I have good news and bad news."

Bad news? Ike knew what that meant—another missed episode of Gilligan's Island.

"The good news is you already understand the basic concepts of annuities. The bad news is what we're here to discuss today, equity-indexed annuities, are just as confusing as what we talked about last time."

Ike sighed, "OK, what is an equity-indexed annuity, and why is it more important than Gilligan's Island?"

Penny winced.

Lotta began her explanation, "An equity-indexed annuity is similar to the fixed annuities we discussed a few weeks ago in that they are contracts issued and guaranteed by insurance companies and, like fixed annuities, are not securities products. Although they aren't regulated by the Securities and Exchange Commission or the Financial Industry Regulatory Authority, they are regulated by state insurance departments,"

Penny was confused. "I thought you told us that equities meant the same thing as stocks?"

"Generally, when we talk about equity, or ownership related to investing, it does mean stock, and you're right, that relates to securities. But the odd thing about equity-indexed annuities is that although they claim to participate in a stock-market index, they're not actually invested in the stock market."

Penny felt even more confused.

"Let me try to explain how it works," Lotta said. "The idea behind indexed annuities is that the owner can have some growth potential linked to the stock market with no risk of principal loss."

At this point Ike piped up, "Wait a second—that sounds too good to be true. You mean if I put money into one of those things, I can't lose?"

"Not exactly," Lotta said, "There are ways you could end up with less money than you started with. You'll see how it works as we continue our discussion."

"Ha!" Ike muttered, "I knew it."

"Here's how they work: When you give the insurance company your money--the premium--they offer you protection against down markets while giving you some of the growth of a particular index; the S&P 500, for instance. Indexed annuities can also offer certain levels of guaranteed income through riders, similar to the variable annuity riders we discussed last time you were here."

"So if the insurance company guarantees no loss, what's the risk?" asked Penny.

"Well," answered Lotta, "for one thing, the guarantee is only as strong as the insurance company. Although it's rare for an insurance company to go belly-up, it has happened. Also, once you turn your money over to the insurance company, you can't get all of it back right away. As we discussed earlier, annuities have surrender charges. In the case of indexed annuities, these can sometimes extend for as long as ten years or more. It's also important for you to understand how growth is calculated in an equity-index annuity."

Ike hoped the length of the appointment wouldn't grow too much.

Lotta continued, "To determine how the insurance company calculates the return, it's important to understand how the index is tracked, as well as how much of the return of the index is credited to you. Caps, participation rates, and spreads can reduce your return potential, sometimes significantly. First, the insurance company looks at how much the index changes. They may measure the change from month to month, over six months, annually, or even a longer period.

"Wouldn't that mean they might miss a period of growth that happens between the points they're looking at?" asked Ike.

"Exactly. Not only that, but they may not credit the total amount of growth. For example, if they assess a cap-rate of 4%, you'll only get 4% credited to your account, even if the index went up 9%. Also, indexed annuities don't usually count dividends in their index-growth calculations, so you don't actually get the full upside of the market. Another way growth can be limited is through the annuity's participation rate. This is the percentage of the index's return the insurance company credits to the annuity, typically ranging from 80% to 100%. For example, if the market went up 6% and the annuity's participation rate was 80%, a 4.8% return (80% of the gain) would be credited. Most indexed annuities that have a participation rate also have a cap, which in our example would limit the credited return to 4% instead of 4.8%."

"So are these the kinds of things covered in all that fine-print in the brochures?" inquired Penny.

"Yes, and that's not all. An indexed annuity might assess a spread, margin, or asset fee. These are percentage fees that may be subtracted from the gain in the index linked to the annuity. For example, if an index gained 12% and the spread fee was 4%, then the gain credited to the annuity would be 8%. One more thing, sometimes insurance companies have the flexibility to lower participations rates, lower the cap, or increase the spreads."

"Wouldn't that reduce the annuity's growth even more?" Ike shook his head.

"Quite likely," Lotta replied.

"Wow," marveled Penny, "with all those limitations, why would anyone want an indexed annuity?"

"Sometimes people are willing to trade upside potential for guarantees, although I tend to agree with you—I have found very few times when equity-indexed annuities are a better choice than variable annuities, fixed annuities, mutual funds or a combination of those three. Remember, though, no two investors are alike. Usually, if you hear some kind of investment is 'always good' or 'always bad,' significant research is needed to get to the truth."

"It's like saying a Ford is always better than a Chevy," added Ike, "a Corvette is better than an F-150 if you want speed, but try hauling a dead moose in your 'Vette!"

"Well, I guess so," said Lotta.

Once again, you've sure given us a lot to think about," sighed Penny, "I hope we can remember it all!"

"You can always call me for a refresher course," Lotta assured her.

"Yeah," Ike thought to himself, "I can't wait to hear all this again."

Chapter 16
WHAT A LOVELY WAY OF SAYING HOW MUCH YOU LOVE ME
THE CYCLE REPEATS

Numbers always bored Ike. He didn't like math in grade school and he didn't like math now.

What he discovered, however, was when he spent time with Penny planning their financial future, it brought them closer together. Actually, it didn't really affect Ike. What it did was help Penny feel that, just perhaps, she hadn't made a huge mistake in marrying him.

Penny craved security, and when Ike seemed interested in financial planning, it made her feel more secure. That, in turn, made her feel closer to Ike. That, in turn, made her feel more like cuddling with Ike.

That, in turn, made Ike react the way God intended for men to react to cuddling.

A few weeks following their last meeting with Lotta, Ike noticed Penny had a certain glow.

Being male, he had no idea what it meant.

A few days later Penny emerged from the bathroom

holding what Ike assumed was part of a chemistry set. She was absolutely gleeful.

"Ike," she exclaimed, "the test is positive!"

Ike struggled to remember whether when it came to medical results "positive" was good and "negative" bad, or the other way around.

Penny didn't wait for Ike to stop looking confused, "We're having a baby!" she cried, "I'm pregnant!"

Ike was stunned. "How in the world did that happen?" Then it hit him, "It was that discussion I had with Penny about annuities! Well, that and the romantic dinner…"

"Oh, Ike—I can't wait to start planning for our child's financial future. Do you think we should buy a life insurance policy, open a brokerage account, or start a 529 college savings plan?"

The more Ike thought about being a dad, the more excited he felt. Then it hit him--the realization of the responsibilities of parenting. In addition to learning how to change a diaper, Ike knew he'd better bone-up on financial planning, but where to start?

"Well," Ike said to Penny, "what did our parents do?